AF228346

Jimmy Carter

Jimmy Carter

A Presidential Life of Service

ERIC BRAUN

LERNER PUBLICATIONS ◆ MINNEAPOLIS

Lerner Publications Company
An imprint of Lerner Publishing Group, Inc.
241 First Avenue North
Minneapolis, MN 55401 USA

For reading levels and more information, look up this title at www.lernerbooks.com.

Image credits: Mercer University/Wikimedia Commons (PD), p. 2; Wikimedia Commons (PD), p. 6, 19; AP Photo, pp. 8, 9, 10, 13, 27, 28, 31, 32, 34, 37; mauritius images GmbH/Alamy Stock Photo, p. 12; Keystone Pictures USA/ZUMAPRESS.com/Alamy Stock Photo, pp. 14,16; gregobagel/iStock/Getty Images, p. 15; Bettmann/Getty Images, p. 17; US Navy/Wikimedia Commons (PD), p. 18; Everett Collection Historical/Alamy Stock Photo, pp. 20, 22; AP Photo/ Bill Achatz, p. 21; AP Photo/Billy Downs, p. 23; AP Photo/Horace Cort, pp. 24, 25; AP Photo/ CHARLES KELLY, p. 26; AP Photo/Bob Scott, p. 30 (top); AP Photo/DR, p. 30 (bottom); AP Photo/John Duricka, p. 36; EQRoy/Shutterstock.com, p. 38; BJOERN SIGURDSON/AFP via Getty Images, p. 39; AP Photo/Matt Rourke, p. 40; AP Photo/Star Max, p. 41.

Cover: Chris Graythen/Getty Images.

Main body text set in Rotis Serif Std 55 Regular. Typeface provided by Adobe Systems.

Editor: Brianna Kaiser **Designer:** Mary Ross
Lerner team: Sue Marquis

Library of Congress Cataloging-in-Publication Data

Names: Braun, Eric, 1971– author.
Title: Jimmy Carter : a presidential life of service / Eric Braun.
Description: Minneapolis : Lerner Publications, [2024] | Series: Gateway biographies | Includes
    bibliographical references and index. | Audience: Ages 9–14 | Audience: Grades 4–6 |
    Summary: "Jimmy Carter served as the 39th US president from 1977 to 1981. In 2002 he
    won the Nobel Peace Prize. Read about Carter's journey from a peanut farm in Georgia to the
    White House"– Provided by publisher.
Identifiers: LCCN 2021003100 (print) | LCCN 2021003101 (ebook) | ISBN 9781728404509 (library
    binding) | ISBN 9781728418209 (ebook)
Subjects: LCSH: Carter, Jimmy, 1924-–Juvenile literature. | Presidents–United States–
    Biography–Juvenile literature. | Ex-presidents–United States–Biography–Juvenile literature.
    | Plains (Ga.)–Biography–Juvenile literature.
Classification: LCC E873 .B73 2024 (print) | LCC E873 (ebook) | DDC 973.926092 [B]–dc23

LC record available at https://lccn.loc.gov/2021003100
LC ebook record available at https://lccn.loc.gov/2021003101

Manufactured in the United States of America
1-48508-49022-10/9/2023

TABLE OF CONTENTS

Official White House photograph of Jimmy Carter in 1977

After four years of campaigning for president, only one thing was left to do: wait. So Jimmy Carter settled into a large suite on the fifteenth floor of the Omni Hotel in Atlanta, Georgia. He and his wife, Rosalynn Carter, were surrounded by their four children, campaign workers, and advisers. Three televisions, each tuned to one of the three major TV networks, stood before them. Carter took his wife's hand.

It was election day, November 2, 1976. Earlier that day, Carter had cast his own ballot in his hometown of Plains, Georgia. He had made his final campaign appearances, and now they watched the results come in.

The Secret Service had closed off the entire floor of the hotel for Carter and his campaign workers, and people hung out all around the halls and rooms. They walked through Carter's suite, sometimes standing in front of the TVs, and he politely asked them to move so he could see. Excited and nervous chatter filled the air.

On November 2, 1976, Carter supporters wait at the World Congress Center in Atlanta, Georgia, for election results.

As results slowly came in, news anchors began to announce how each state had voted. Results from the East Coast came in first and moved west following the time zones. As expected, Carter took most of the states in the East. Each time a state was announced in his favor, whoops and hollers rose up in the suite. Many on the Carter team began to feel confident.

But as the night wore on, the race tightened. Kansas was announced for Carter's opponent, President Gerald Ford. That state was soon followed by Ford wins in Nebraska, Colorado, Utah, Wyoming, and many more. Everyone had expected Ford to take most of the western states. Still, the race was tight.

Carter spent much of the evening on the phone. He called supporters to thank them. He called politicians in various states to get their opinions of how the night was going.

More and more people filled the suite. Coretta King, widow of the civil rights leader Martin Luther King Jr., showed up with her father-in-law, Martin Luther King Sr. The race was so close that the networks had to be cautious about announcing results. They wanted to be sure their reports were accurate. Just after midnight, CBS called Oregon for Carter. Not long after, the network's anchor, Walter Cronkite, had to take it back, saying the state was too close to call. Oregon eventually went to Ford.

Soon some of the states with the most electoral votes were being called. New York and Pennsylvania went to Carter. Michigan went to Ford. Carter was closing in on a win. Television stations showed thousands of cheering Carter supporters in a convention center attached to the Omni Hotel. Finally, Mississippi was called for Carter, pushing him over the number of electoral votes needed to win. When the major news networks announced Carter's victory early in the morning, the suite exploded with celebratory

Carter and his wife, Rosalynn, embrace after his third presidential debate on October 22, 1976.

yells, cheers, and hugs. James Earl Carter Jr. was the new president of the United States.

Carter went downstairs to address his thrilled supporters at four in the morning. "We have a great nation as you know, and sometimes in the past we've been disappointed at our own government," Carter said to the crowd. "But I think it's time . . . to unify our nation, to make it great once again." After his speech, the Carters went back to Plains, arriving just as dawn was breaking. Hundreds of supporters greeted him at his campaign headquarters. They'd waited for him all night.

When Carter launched his campaign for president four years earlier, he was the governor of Georgia. But he was virtually unknown in national politics. With this lack of fame came a lack of support from others in his party and a lack of money, all of which he needed for successful campaigning. Carter was an obscure peanut farmer from a

Carter, Rosalynn, and their daughter, Amy, wave to supporters in celebration of his presidential victory.

tiny town in the South.

Every election is emotional, and every presidential election is historically important. Still, to his supporters, Carter's win seemed to carry even more weight than usual. The South had not held any significant national political power since before the Civil War (1861–1865). Now a small-town southerner had been elected president. Even more important, Carter had put civil rights at the center of his campaign. He gave people hope that America could be unified in more ways than one.

FARM GROWN

In 1920 Bessie Lillian Gordy moved to Plains, Georgia. The town had only about five hundred residents, but it had the Wise Sanitarium, the hospital where she started her nurse's training. She then completed her training at Grady Memorial Hospital in Atlanta.

Three years later, she was working at Wise as a registered nurse when she married James Earl Carter. On October 1, 1924, she gave birth to their son, James Earl Carter Jr. The Carters went on to buy a farm in Archery, an even smaller community nearby. They would eventually have three more children: Gloria, Ruth, and Billy.

The farmhouse where Jimmy grew up had no electricity or running water. The only heat came from the kitchen stove and some fireplaces. His bedroom was far from all

This picture of downtown Plains was taken in 2013.

of these, making the cold winters miserable. But Jimmy remembered his childhood fondly. "The early years of my life on the farm were full and enjoyable, isolated but not lonely," he said later. "We always had enough to eat, no economic hardship, but no money to waste. We felt close to nature, close to members of our family, and close to God."

Jimmy worked on the farm from a young age. He learned to do many skills with his hands, including woodworking and blacksmithing. At five years old, Jimmy began to earn his own income by harvesting peanuts on the farm. He washed, boiled, and salted peanuts, and divided them into paper bags. After breakfast, he walked into Plains and sold his bags for five cents apiece, earning around a dollar a day.

Years later, he used his savings to buy five cotton bales. After reselling the cotton bales, he used his earnings to

Carter, age 6 (*left*), and his sister Gloria (*right*) in 1931 in Plains

buy some houses. He rented out the houses and rode his bike to each house to collect the monthly rent. Jimmy kept careful records of his expenses and income.

The Carters were one of only two white families in Archery. Everyone else was Black. Before Jimmy started school, all his friends were Black. After starting school in Plains at the age of six, Jimmy made friends with other white kids there. But he kept his Black friends from

THE PASTURE GATE

When Jimmy was about fourteen, he was working in a field with two of his Black friends. The three of them were about to step through a gate in the pasture when the other two boys stepped back to let Jimmy go through first. Jimmy didn't understand why they did that—at first, he thought they may have been playing some kind of trick on him. Later, he realized that his friends' parents had taught them to defer to white people as a strategy to keep themselves safe from racism. The incident became a powerful early lesson for Jimmy on unfair treatment based on race.

Archery.

Jimmy's father believed strongly that Black and white people should be segregated, or separated. But his mother always treated their Black friends and neighbors as equals. Jimmy was also introduced to politics from an early age. His father resented federal government programs, which he saw as getting needlessly involved with people's individual affairs. Jimmy and his family listened to the major political parties' conventions on the radio.

Navy Man

When Jimmy was young, he began to exchange letters with his uncle, Tom Gordy, a radio operator in the US Navy. Gordy told Jimmy of his adventures in Australia, Japan, China, the Philippines, and other countries. Jimmy began thinking of a life in the navy.

As Jimmy neared high school graduation, his parents made it clear that they wanted him to go to college. Jimmy's father had only a tenth-grade education, and he wanted more for his son. But college was expensive.

Carter in his US Naval Academy uniform

Carter began his studies at the US Naval Academy in 1943.

One option was the US Naval Academy in Annapolis, Maryland. It was hard to get in, but the education was free. After graduation, the graduate would serve as an officer in the navy. It sounded like a win-win for Jimmy.

He did not get into the academy after high school, however, so he began his college career at Georgia Southwestern State University. During his freshman year, the Japanese bombed Pearl Harbor, and the United States entered World War II (1939–1945).

In 1943 Carter reapplied and was admitted to the academy, and he began his studies in July. Studying naval engineering, he learned all about how ships and their equipment were constructed and operated. He was also an avid reader. He studied many topics in addition to his normal academic load, including history, literature, and aviation.

As part of his training, Carter took summer trips aboard naval ships. One year he sailed to Trinidad aboard an old battleship, the USS *New York*. He was at sea in 1945 when President Harry Truman announced that

the United States had dropped an atomic bomb on Hiroshima, Japan. Days after the US dropped a second atomic bomb on Nagasaki, Japan surrendered, effectively ending World War II.

While Carter was in the academy, he began dating Rosalynn Smith. Smith had grown up near the Carters in Georgia. The two went out when he was home for vacations. Carter later described Smith as "remarkably beautiful, almost painfully shy, obviously intelligent, and yet unrestrained in our discussions."

Carter asked Smith to marry him, but she turned him down. She had promised her late father that she would graduate from college before marrying. She finally accepted Carter's proposal after graduating from junior college, and the two were married on July 7, 1946. Their first child, John, was born in July the following year.

Meanwhile, Carter had graduated from the academy and was commissioned as an officer in the navy. He worked on battleships for two years. As an electronics officer, he got to work with the newest technology in the armed forces. Once again, he dedicated himself to learning everything he could.

Carter also developed an interest in politics. He admired Truman for his views on economic issues and his commitment to racial equality. He also admired Henry Wallace, who had served as Franklin Delano Roosevelt's vice president and was critical of racial segregation. Truman and Wallace were both running for president in 1948. Carter planned to vote for Truman. But many of Carter's surrounding officers planned to vote for another of Truman's opponents, Republican Thomas Dewey. Carter decided to keep quiet about his own views.

Carter and Rosalynn married in 1946. They went on to have three sons: John, James, and Jeffrey.

In 1948 Carter applied and was accepted for a submarine assignment. He trained for six months, learning how the ships dived and sailed, about their torpedoes, guns, and propulsion, and about submarine seamanship techniques. He also had to practice escaping from underwater disasters. As an officer, he had to be an expert on all areas of the subs.

After submarine school, Carter was assigned to the USS *Pomfret*, a standard World War II sub. He later

Carter worked on the USS *Pomfret* after submarine school. Here, the USS *Pomfret* sails in 1951.

Carter commanded the USS *K-1*.

commanded the USS *K-1*, or "Killer 1." In 1952 he began working with the navy's new, highly secret nuclear submarine program. By then the Carters had had two more boys, James III (nicknamed Chip) and Jeffrey.

As he had done so many times before, Carter immersed himself in learning. Nuclear energy, which powered the sub, was complicated and dangerous. In addition to his training, he studied nuclear physics. By the time he had completed his education, he and his team were among the people in the world most knowledgeable about nuclear technology.

ENTERING POLITICS

Carter's father fell seriously ill with pancreatic cancer in April 1953. He was going to die. Carter received permission to visit his father in the summer. He sat with him during his final days and talked about navy life. His father told Carter about life on the farm. Through their talks, Carter learned that his father was very active in the community. He was helping to educate farmers on agricultural practices and to develop technical colleges.

After his father died in July, Carter began to rethink

his future. He loved his life in the navy. If he stayed, he could rise in the naval ranks. But he admired what his father had done to improve his community. And he missed life on the farm. After thinking it over, Carter resigned from the navy and returned to Plains.

Carter found himself picking cotton and curing peanuts, just as he had when he was a child. But running the business of the farm was a massive job that he knew little about. He later said, "My wide-ranging and expanding responsibilities made my previous navy life—even helping to design and build an original nuclear power plant—seem simple."

Slowly, Carter expanded the business in different ways, including by selling peanut seeds and fertilizer. By the early 1960s, he had started a successful farming warehouse that supplied farmers with anything they needed.

Carter soon became involved in local political issues.
He learned that the schools for Black children were poorly
outfitted, especially compared to the schools for white
children. Students shared old, out-of-date books. They had
no music or art instruction. They met in churches and
homes because they didn't have school buildings. They
didn't even have enough desks or chairs.

In 1954 the Supreme Court ruling in *Brown v. Board
of Education* had established that schools should be
integrated, or open to all races. But in Carter's part of

In the 1950s, schools across the country started to integrate after the ruling of
Brown v. Board of Education.

Even after *Brown v. Board of Education* ruled that schools should be integrated, some schools in Georgia resisted. This image of a segregated classroom in Georgia was taken six years after the Supreme Court case.

Georgia, the law was being ignored. Through his church, Carter participated in a steering committee to encourage integration. But as the Carters grew more vocal about ending segregation, many in his community became angry with them. Carter even had to install his own gas pump because a white gas station owner refused to sell him gas.

Some white men pressured Carter to join the White Citizens' Council, an organization that believed white people were superior to Black people, and that was opposed to racial integration. But Carter refused. This caused even more anger toward him. People spread

Along with schools, many public places were segregated in the 1950s. Here, a man protests hotel segregation in Atlanta.

rumors among his customers that he was a Communist, and some customers stopped buying supplies from his warehouse.

As the years passed, however, Carter gained a reputation for being a strong community member and leader. He became the county board of education chair and district governor of fifty-six Lions Clubs in his area. He also held state leadership positions in various farming and seed business organizations. Slowly, local schools began to integrate, and most of Carter's warehouse customers returned.

In 1962 a seat in the state senate opened up, and Carter made a last-minute decision to run as a Democrat. He knew he could do more good for people in a government position. Though he had entered the race late, he was able to overcome that disadvantage with his strong connections in his community and throughout much of the state.

On October 16, 1962, election day, Carter learned that Joe Hurst, the Democratic Party chair in Quitman County, was at a polling place pressuring people to vote for Carter's opponent Homer Moore. If people voted for Carter,

Two ministers lead a protest march in Birmingham, Alabama, a year before the Civil Rights Act passed.

Hurst threw their ballots away. Carter ended up losing the close race. Angry about the corrupt voting in Quitman, he hired a lawyer and contested the election. Eventually a judge overturned the results due to fraud and held a new one. This time, Carter won.

As state senator, Carter worked hard to continue to integrate and improve education for all people in his state. With his knowledge of farming and agriculture, he also served on the senate's agricultural committee.

In 1964 the Civil Rights Act passed. The act, which ended segregation in public places and banned employment discrimination, further inflamed racial tension in the South. Carter continued to work for racial equality, but he was not outspoken on the issue because he did not want to anger the many segregationists in his state. He needed their support. His silence helped him get elected to a second term.

Higher Office

Carter planned to run for the US Congress in 1966 against Bo Callaway, a Republican who had recently left the Democratic Party because of segregation. Callaway was more pro-segregation than most Democrats were. Carter had clashed with Callaway several times and badly wanted to defeat him. But suddenly Callaway dropped out of the congressional race to run for governor of Georgia.

Though the state had not had a Republican governor since 1872, Callaway was favored to win. Carter decided to switch to the governor's race as well. But he lost the

Bo Callaway (*left*) and Lester Maddox (*right*) have a debate in 1966 ahead of the Georgia election for governor.

On April 3, 1970, Carter announces his candidacy for governor.

Democratic primary. The Democratic candidate, Lester Maddox, a segregationist, won the office. Carter was deeply disappointed.

He returned to his work on the farm and at his warehouse. But he planned to run for governor again in 1970. He spent the years leading up to the election traveling around the state after work. He participated in public events, made speeches, and met voters. He built relationships with influential people in business and politics in the state. Carter returned home late at night, only to get up the next day to work and travel again.

In the summer of 1970, Carter's family went on the

road to campaign for him. Carter's friend David Rabhan flew him around the state in a twin-engine Cessna airplane. Carter spoke at churches, high schools, colleges, and many events. He ran a more conservative campaign this time, knowing that he had little chance to win a statewide election as a liberal. To conservative audiences, he even praised George Wallace, the racist segregationist governor of Alabama. Carter painted his Democratic opponent, Carl Sanders, as wealthy and out of touch with regular working people. He played up his own working-class background as a way to relate to voters.

His tactics worked. Carter won a tight Democratic primary and went on to easily defeat his Republican opponent in the general election. On January 12, 1971, he was sworn in as the governor of Georgia. "I thank you all for making it possible for me to be here on what is certainly the greatest day of my life," Carter said during his inaugural address. He went on to

Carter smiles during the Democratic campaign for governor of Georgia.

Carter (*right*) is sworn in as governor of Georgia on January 12, 1971.

stress the need for education for all and to address racial discrimination.

Carter also used his speech to repay Rabhan for all the help Rabhan gave him during the campaign. Near the end of the election, Rabhan told Carter to get a piece of paper and pencil and write down what he was about to say. "The time for racial discrimination is over in Georgia," Rabhan said. "This is what I want you to say when you are inaugurated."

Carter followed through. When he spoke that day in January, he echoed his friend's words. "I say to you quite frankly that the time for racial discrimination is over . . . No poor, rural, weak, or Black person should ever again have to bear the additional burden of being deprived of the opportunity of an education, a job, or simple justice."

Many in the audience were shocked by Carter's

message, especially the segregationists who had supported him. It was a bold statement that seemed to signal a new, more progressive future for the South and for Georgia in particular. Because Carter had presented himself as conservative in his campaign but was taking progressive measures in office, some of his supporters thought he ran dishonestly.

Indeed, civil rights were one of Carter's highest priorities as governor. He made reforms that provided equal state aid to all schools in Georgia, whether in wealthy or poor areas. He worked to provide greater educational opportunities for people convicted of crimes and to provide funds for prison reform. He appointed Black judges and board members and hired Black employees.

Carter also worked hard to bring increased business to his state. He visited business leaders in foreign countries and persuaded them to invest in Georgia. He even went to Hollywood and New York and persuaded movie producers to make movies in his state.

Carter met with many Democratic presidential candidates during the 1972 election. He wanted to make as many connections as he could to help him in a future run for national office.

George McGovern was chosen as the Democratic candidate for president. Carter knew that as a liberal, McGovern would have trouble getting support in the South. By the time McGovern lost to Republican Richard Nixon in November, Carter had started planning his 1976 run for president.

Running for President

Carter's biggest obstacle to getting elected president was his lack of popularity outside of Georgia. Other candidates were considered favorites to win the Democratic nomination, including Governor Wallace of Alabama and Governor Jerry Brown of California. Carter spent a lot of time traveling the nation, speaking at various events, and making connections with voters as well as influential people in the Democratic Party.

Carter also didn't have much money to fund his campaign. When his term as governor ended in 1975, he began to travel the nation with his press secretary, Jody Powell. The two usually stayed in the homes of

Carter shakes hands with members of the crowd at a presidential rally in Portland, Oregon, in 1976.

Carter spent time making connections with voters when running for governor and president. Here, Carter greets supporters in 1971.

supporters or shared a small hotel room. They hosted press events where Carter could meet reporters and speak about his positions on issues. But early on, they had trouble getting reporters to show up. Nobody took his candidacy seriously.

Positioning himself as a moderate alternative to the liberal Brown and conservative Wallace, Carter began to gain support. His operation grew, with his wife and their sons—as well as many Georgia volunteers known as the Peanut Brigade—traveling and speaking on his behalf.

When the primary season ramped up, Carter won upset victories in both Iowa and New Hampshire. He then took several more states. As it became clear he would be the Democratic candidate for president, he chose a running mate for vice president. Carter chose Walter Mondale, a US senator from Minnesota.

Carter's opponent was Gerald Ford, who had been vice president for Nixon. When Nixon resigned amid the Watergate scandal, Ford succeeded him. Ford emphasized his experience in national politics during the campaign.

Carter and Walter Mondale attend the Democratic National Convention on July 15, 1976.

In contrast, Carter ran as a political outsider who could bring a fresh voice to the presidency. On election night the race was a dead heat. Both candidates and their teams stayed up late watching the results as they were announced on national television. Carter carried twenty-three states with 297 electoral votes, while Ford won twenty-seven states with 240 electoral votes. The electoral vote was the closest since 1916.

Electoral College

Presidential elections in the United States are determined by the Electoral College, a body of 538 electors who cast their votes for their respective states. A presidential candidate needs a majority, or at least 270 electoral votes, to become president.

Each state is given a number of electors that matches its number of congressional representatives. That number is determined by a state's population. For example, California, the most populous state, has two senators and fifty-three representatives, giving it fifty-five electors in the Electoral College. In forty-eight states, the candidate who wins the most votes in the state gets all of that state's electoral votes. In Maine and Nebraska, the votes are divided so that the winner of each congressional district gets that district's vote.

The Electoral College was established to give states with smaller populations more power. But opponents of the Electoral College argue that it makes the votes of people in more populated areas less valuable. In several elections, the candidate who earned fewer votes still managed to gain more Electoral College votes and win the election in spite of having less popular support.

President of the United States

Carter was inaugurated as the thirty-ninth president of the United States on January 20, 1977. "The phrase 'President Carter' was startling to me, but I was ready and eager to assume the responsibility," Carter later said. That night the Carters attended eleven parties. His first official act as president was to pardon those who had evaded the draft during the Vietnam War (1955–1975).

Carter faced serious national problems when he took office. The country was deep in an energy crisis, a serious shortage of energy. Carter urged all Americans to conserve energy. He established the US Department of Energy in 1977 to guide the country's energy policy. The US was also still recovering from a deep economic recession, or a period of economic decline. In response, Carter proposed the Public Works Employment Act of 1977, which put money into public projects. It created many jobs and raised the median income for US families. But these gains were later erased by the worsening energy crisis.

On January 20, 1977, Carter (*bottom right*) takes the oath of office.

Just as he had as a state senator and governor, Carter prioritized education. Working with Congress, he created the US Department of Education in 1979 to establish federal policy for education and to provide federal assistance to US schools. Carter also expanded the Head Start early childhood education program.

Less successful was Carter's proposed plan for universal national health care. He believed that access to quality health care was a basic right. His plan passed the Senate but not the House, and the bill died.

One major achievement of Carter's presidency was the 1978 peace agreement he negotiated between Israel and Egypt. The agreement attempted to settle the long-running conflict between Israel and its Arab neighbors in the Middle East. Carter met with various leaders in the Middle East and eventually invited Egyptian leader

Anwar Sadat and Israeli prime minister Menachem Begin to the US for negotiations.

Carter, Sadat, and Begin met at Camp David, the presidential retreat in Maryland. Though the negotiations were tense and at times seemed hopeless, Carter kept the talks going. Eventually, Sadat and Begin signed a peace treaty. Carter later wrote a book about the experience called *Keeping Faith: Memoirs of a President*. He considered the agreement his greatest success as president.

However, Carter would soon face another huge challenge: the Iran hostage crisis. Early in his term, Carter had pledged to continue positive relations with Iran. But in 1979, Ayatollah Ruhollah Khomeini—a politician and cleric—led a revolution against the sitting

Carter (*center*) and members of his cabinet meet on January 29, 1977, to discuss the energy crisis.

Sadat (*left*), Carter (*center*), and Begin (*right*), announce that an agreement was reached during their meetings at Camp David.

Iranian government. The revolutionaries had many motives, but one motive was that they thought the Iranian government was too beholden to Western powers such as the United States.

On November 4, 1979, revolutionary militants took fifty-two American diplomats and citizens hostage at the US Embassy in Tehran, the capital of Iran. Carter tried to negotiate their release through diplomacy. But as the weeks dragged on, he ordered American special forces to begin practicing for a rescue mission.

At first, most Americans approved of Carter's handling of the crisis. Then, in April 1980, Carter officially ordered a rescue mission. The mission failed badly, as eight US soldiers were killed. Carter's approval polling went way down as a result, and the crisis became a major theme of his reelection campaign.

Life After the Presidency

Before the general election of 1980, Senator Ted Kennedy of Massachusetts challenged Carter for the Democratic nomination. Kennedy was much more liberal than Carter and resented Carter's presidency. Though Carter eventually secured the nomination to run for reelection, Kennedy's campaign hurt Carter.

Carter's Republican challenger in 1980 was Ronald Reagan, a former Hollywood actor and governor of California. With the Iran hostage and energy crises as backdrops, Reagan ran as a fierce conservative.

The Carters established the Carter Center in Atlanta in 1982.

Reagan believed that
government should play only
a very small role in people's
lives, whereas Carter believed
government's role was to
help people who needed
it. In the election, Reagan
swept the southern states,
most of which had supported
Carter four years earlier. In
all, Carter lost one of the
most lopsided presidential
elections in history. He carried
only six states, a deeply
disappointing defeat.

Carter receives the 2002 Nobel Peace Prize on December 20 in Norway.

In January 1981, just
minutes before Carter's term
ended, the American hostages in Iran were released.
Shortly afterward, the Carters returned to Plains.

Carter was determined to keep helping people once
he was out of politics. In 1982 the Carters established
the Carter Center to advance human rights worldwide.
The center strives to fight deadly disease and to promote
health and democracy. It also helps countries in conflict
come to peaceful agreements.

Through the center, Carter negotiated peaceful
resolutions to many international problems. In 1994
Carter traveled to North Korea to negotiate discussions

with the US to maintain peace between the two nations. In September 1994 Carter was asked by the general Raoul Cédras to help resolve a governmental crisis in Haiti and avoid an invasion by the United States. Carter informed then president Bill Clinton of the request, and Clinton agreed to send Carter to Haiti. The Carter Center had a long history of working in Haiti to monitor elections, which helped establish Carter as a trusted ally. He successfully negotiated a peaceful transfer of government. In 2002 he received the Nobel Peace Prize for his work through the center as well as the Camp David Accords between Egypt and Israel.

Carter's values of helping those in need and working for social justice aligned with Habitat for Humanity. It helps people to build and improve homes. In 1984 the Carters began working with the charity. They worked in countries around the world to help build, renovate, and repair thousands of homes.

In addition to all he did for social justice, Carter wrote more than twenty books examining his life and events in the United States in his lifetime. His books include *White House Diary* (2010), *A Full Life: Reflections at Ninety* (2015), and *Faith: A Journey for All* (2018).

In February 2023, the Carter Center announced that Carter was beginning hospice at the age of 98. Instead of receiving medical intervention that could prolong his life at a hospital, Carter would spend his final days at home with his family. For Carter's 99th birthday on October 1, friends, family, and admirers celebrated at the Jimmy Carter Presidential Library and Museum in Atlanta. Guests watched video tributes to Carter's life, toured the museum, and ate birthday cake.

Although his presidency ended in 1981, Carter never stopped working and fighting for social justice. His post-presidency was one of the most impactful in US history.

Carter in 2019

IMPORTANT DATES

1924	James Earl Carter Jr. is born on October 1, 1924, to James Earl Carter Sr. and Bessie Lillian Carter.
1943	Carter starts college at the US Naval Academy.
1946	He is commissioned as an officer in the US Navy.
	On July 7, he marries Rosalynn Smith.
1946–1952	His job as a naval officer causes him and his family to move many times throughout the country.
	His three sons are born.
1953	Carter's father dies of cancer.
	Carter resigns from the navy and returns to Plains to run the family farm.
1962	He is elected to the first of two terms in the Georgia Senate.
1967	His fourth child, Amy, is born on October 19.
1970	He is elected governor of Georgia.
1976	He is elected president of the United States on November 2.

1977	He is inaugurated as the thirty-ninth US president on January 20.
1978	He negotiates a peace agreement between Israel and Egypt at Camp David.
1979	He forms the US Department of Education.
	Fifty-two American hostages are taken at the US Embassy in Iran.
1980	An attempt to rescue the hostages in Iran fails.
	Carter loses his bid for reelection.
1981	The hostages are released minutes before Carter's term as president ends.
1982	The Carters establish the Carter Center.
1984	The Carters begin their work with Habitat for Humanity.
2002	He wins the Nobel Peace Prize for his work with the Carter Center.
2023	He begins hospice at home in February.
	On October 1, Carter turns 99 years old.

SOURCE NOTES

10 "1976 Jimmy Carter Victory Speech," YouTube video, 3:10, posted by "theCarbonFreeze," November 5, 2017, https://www.youtube.com/watch?v=c8Qs6q4h7CM.

12 "Jimmy Carter National Historic Site," National Park Service, accessed December 15, 2020, https://www.nps.gov/nr/travel/presidents/jimmy_carter_nhs.html.

16 Jimmy Carter, *A Full Life: Reflections at Ninety* (New York: Simon & Schuster Paperbacks, 2015), 38.

20 Carter, 70.

27 "Governor Jimmy Carter's Inaugural Address—January 12, 1971,"
Jimmy Carter Library, accessed December 10, 2020, https://www
.jimmycarterlibrary.gov/assets/documents/inaugural_address_gov
.pdf.

28 Carter, *A Full Life*, 101.

28 Carter, 101.

33 Carter, 118.

SELECTED BIBLIOGRAPHY

Bourne, Peter G. *Jimmy Carter: A Comprehensive Biography from Plains to Post-Presidency.* New York: Scribner, 1997.

Carter, Jimmy. *A Full Life: Reflections at Ninety.* New York: Simon & Schuster, 2015.

———. *Turning Point: A Candidate, a State, and a Nation Come of Age.* New York: Times Books, 1992.

"Carter Work Project." Habitat for Humanity. Accessed December 15, 2020. https://www.habitat.org/volunteer/build-events/carter-work-project.

"Jimmy Carter." Academy of Achievement. Last modified August 17, 2019. https://achievement.org/achiever/jimmy-carter/.

Pramuk, Jacob. "Former President Jimmy Carter Reveals He Has Cancer." CNBC, August 12, 2015. https://www.cnbc.com/2015/08/12/former-president-jimmy-carter-reveals-he-has-cancer.html.

Witcover, Jules. *Marathon: The Pursuit of the Presidency, 1972–1976.* New York: Viking, 1977.

LEARN MORE

The Carter Center
 https://www.cartercenter.org

Denenberg, Dennis, and Lorraine Roscoe. *60 American Heroes Every Kid Should Meet*. Minneapolis: Lerner Publications, 2023.

Jimmy Carter: From Plains to the White House and Beyond
 https://jimmycarter.info

Schwartz, Heather E. *Joe Biden: From Scranton to the White House*. Minneapolis: Lerner Publications, 2021.

The White House: James Carter
 https://www.whitehouse.gov/about-the-white-house/presidents/james-carter/

Williamson, Justin W. *Operation Eagle Claw 1980: The Disastrous Bid to End the Iran Hostage Crisis*. New York: Bloomsbury, 2020.

INDEX